CURSIVE BEGINNING HANDWRITING WORKBOOK
FOR 2nd – 6th GRADE

The Big Coloring Book to Learn Upper and Lowercase Cursive Writing

that Includes the Alphabet, Seasons, Months, Numbers, Names, Short Words, & Sentences

Dr. Melissa Caudle

"An Award-winning Principal of the Year"

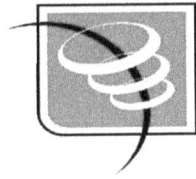

Absolute Author
Publishing House

CHILDREN'S DIVISION

Dedicated to all of my grandchildren.

CURSIVE BEGINNING HANDWRITING WORKBOOK
Copyright 2020
Dr. Melissa Caudle

Publisher: Absolute Author Publishing House
Editor: Dr. Carol Michaels
Cover Designer: MD. Sheikh Shoeb Uddin
Illustrator: Sidra Ayyaz

ISBN: 978-1-951028-87-9

1. Education   2. English as a Second Language   3. Handwriting

Dear Parents and Teachers:

Cursive writing has almost become a lost skill. As a retired educator with more than twenty years, a mother, and grandmother, I know the importance of having fun for children as they learn. Shouldn't all learning? I'm glad you agree.

When my grandchildren informed me that schools no longer taught cursive handwriting, I was horrified. Learning to write cursive is an important skill and research as proven that children who do learn, it impacts their thinking, language, and memory. Repeated studies have proven the connection between the left and right hemispheres of the brain when writing. It is also important that your child has the essential fine motor skills of handwriting and can print each letter before introducing cursive letters. I have outlined this book strategically for your child to use similar learning movements. Here is the order that your child will learn to write cursive letters, both in lower and uppercases, based on fundamental research and like movements.

1. C, A, D, and G
2. H, T, P, E L, F and Q
3. U, I, J, K, R, and S
4. O, B, V, and W
5. M, N, Y, X, and Z

I have carefully constructed this book using sound principles of teaching. Think of this method as teaching a child to write the alphabet one letter at a time, only not in alphabetical order. Your child must practice each letter and master it before moving to the next. That is why I recommend that each child also has Book 2 in this series, *The Big Practice Book for Lined Cursive Writing,* for his or her additional practice.

This cursive handwriting book is divided into three parts, and each part has a coloring book page to encourage engagement.

- Part 1 – *Tracing and Writing the Cursive Alphabet in Lower and Uppercase from A – Z*
- Part 2 – *Cursive Writing Numbers, Colors, Seasons, Months, and Names*
- Part 3 – *Writing Short Words and Sentences in Cursive*

Please remember, writing in cursive is a fun activity, as well as your child learning a new skill. As a reward, encourage your child to color the images throughout the book and as a bonus, the dividers for each part are coloring pages and I have also included several fun activity sheets as bonus fun activities after each one. Please allow children to color and have fun. That is what this book is about – FUN!

Supplies Needed:

#2 Pencil
Crayons, colored pencils, or markers to color each image.
Eraser
Pencil Sharpener

*For added practice, consider purchasing *The Big Practice Book for Lined Cursive Writing.*

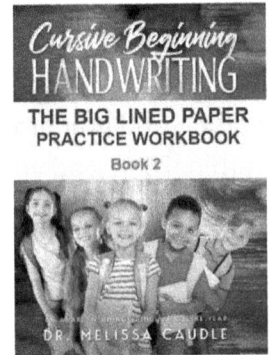

TIPS FOR PARENTS AND TEACHERS

1. When working with your child, monitor their progress, and demonstrate how to trace the letters and then to write them. Children learn by watching.
2. Make sure there is sufficient light in the area.
3. Always use the lined cursive paper when teaching your child. It is challenging for them to use unlined paper or regular lined paper used in school. It is wise to invest in practice workbook that goes with this book to provide your child with plenty of space to practice writing in cursive.
4. Make sure that your child is sitting at a table or desk where they can comfortably write and have excellent posture. It is okay if your child wants to move their paper diagonally to create a slant for writing. It is the most natural way. For right-handed children, the paper should be parallel with the child's hand slanted left at about a twenty percent angle. If you have a left-handed child, they will slant their paper to the right. The essential factor is that they are comfortable.

5. With every exercise in this book, have your child trace over the guided arrows, see sample below, for each alphabet or word until they are comfortable before moving to the dot-to-dot letter, followed by independent practice on the lined page area.

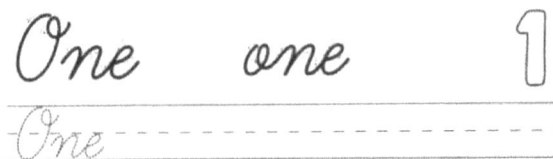

$$One \qquad one \qquad 1$$

Happy cursive writing,

Dr. Melissa Caudle

THE UPPERCASE ALPHABET

Are you ready to learn how to write cursive letters? Let's go! First, you will learn to recognize the uppercase cursive alphabet.

Sing the ABCs as you point to each uppercase cursive letter below?

Now go back and use your pencil, follow the arrows and numbers, and trace each uppercase letter to get the feel of the motion it takes to write in cursive.

THE LOWERCASE CURSIVE ALPHABET

Are you ready to learn how to write cursive letters? Let's go! First, you will learn to recognize the uppercase cursive alphabet.

Sing the ABCs as you point to each uppercase cursive letter below

a   b   c   d

e   f   g   h

i   j   k   l

m   n   o   p

q   r   s   t

u   v   w   x

y   z

Now go back and using your pencil, follow the arrows and numbers to trace each lowercase letter.

LEARNING THE MOTIONS FOR CURSIVE WRITING

Now that you are all warmed up, it's time to learn to write in cursive. The first step is to develop your fine motor skills. To begin you will learn to make loops, waves, and angles like these.

HILLS

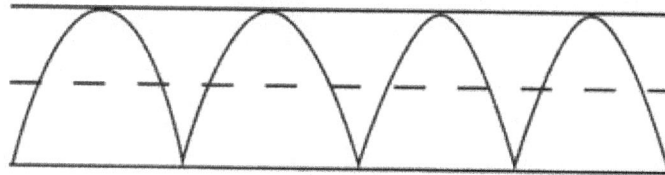

MOUNTAINS

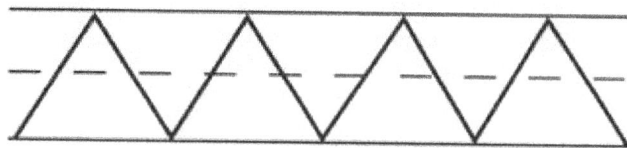

LOOPS

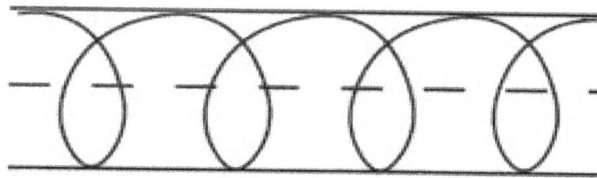

ROLLER COASTER

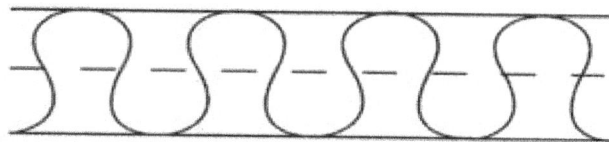

Take your time until you have fluid movements. If you need too, use an extra practice sheet from the practice book. You can also trace over the patterns on the next couple of pages as often as you need to. It is important that you have fluid motions.

Ready? Set. Go!

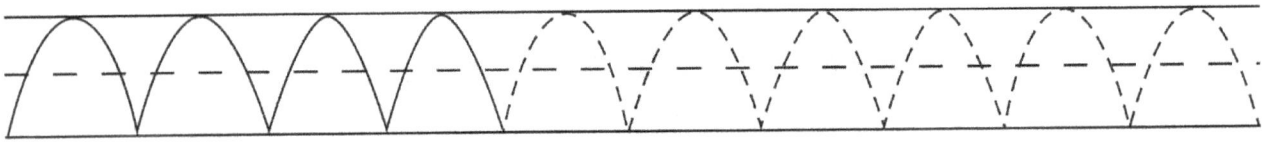

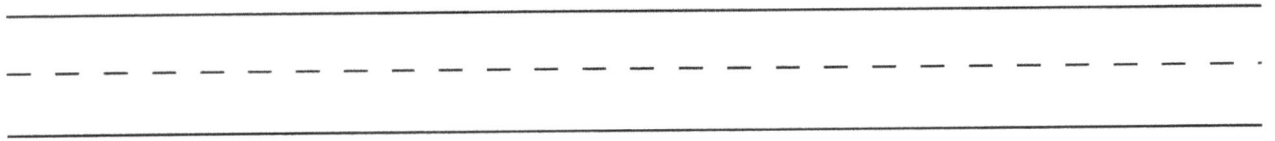

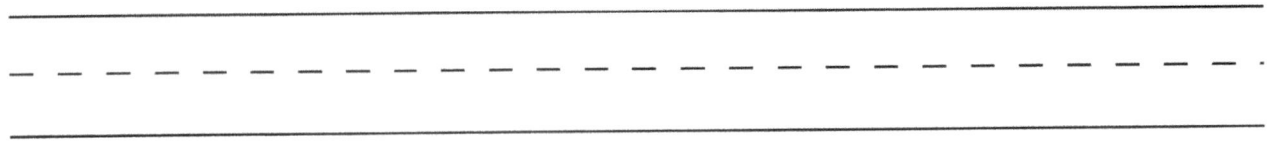

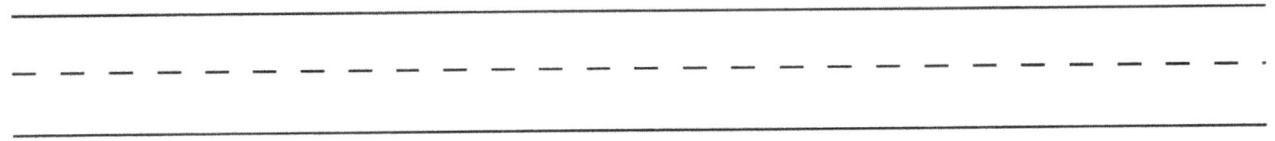

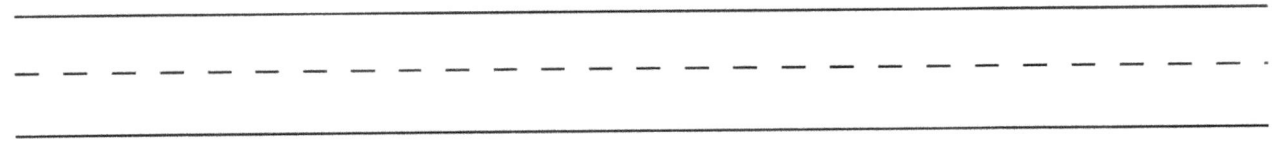

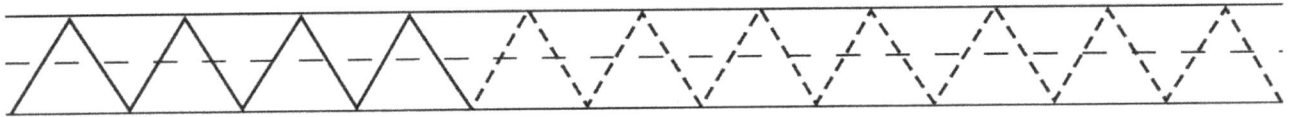

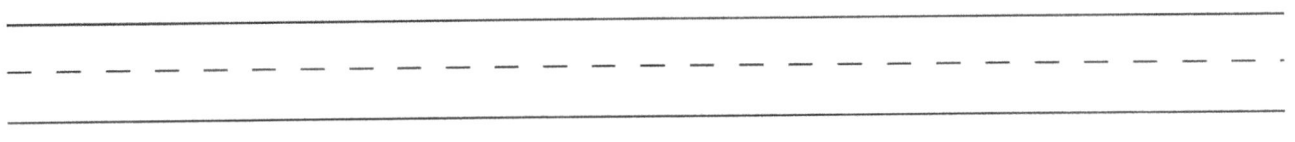

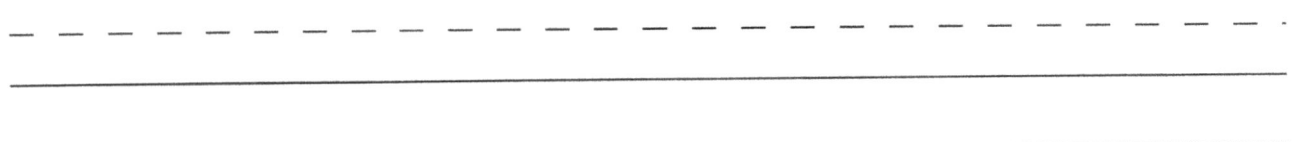

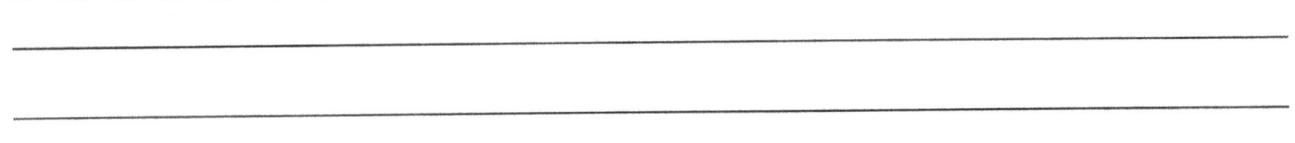

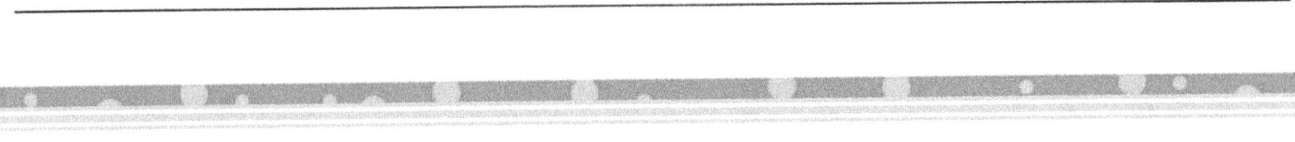

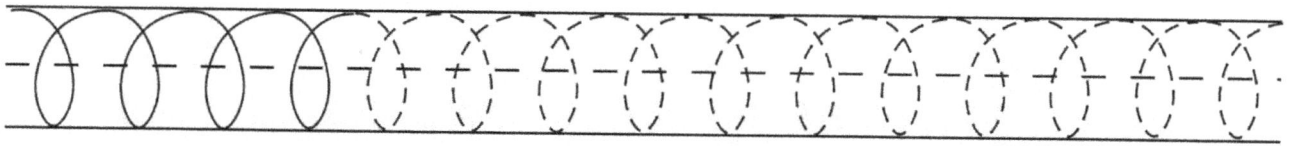

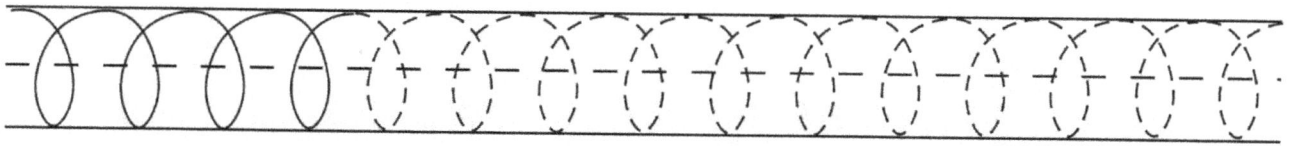

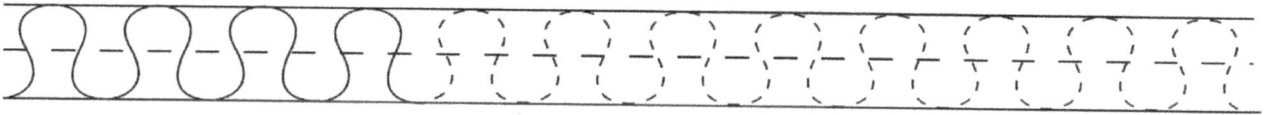

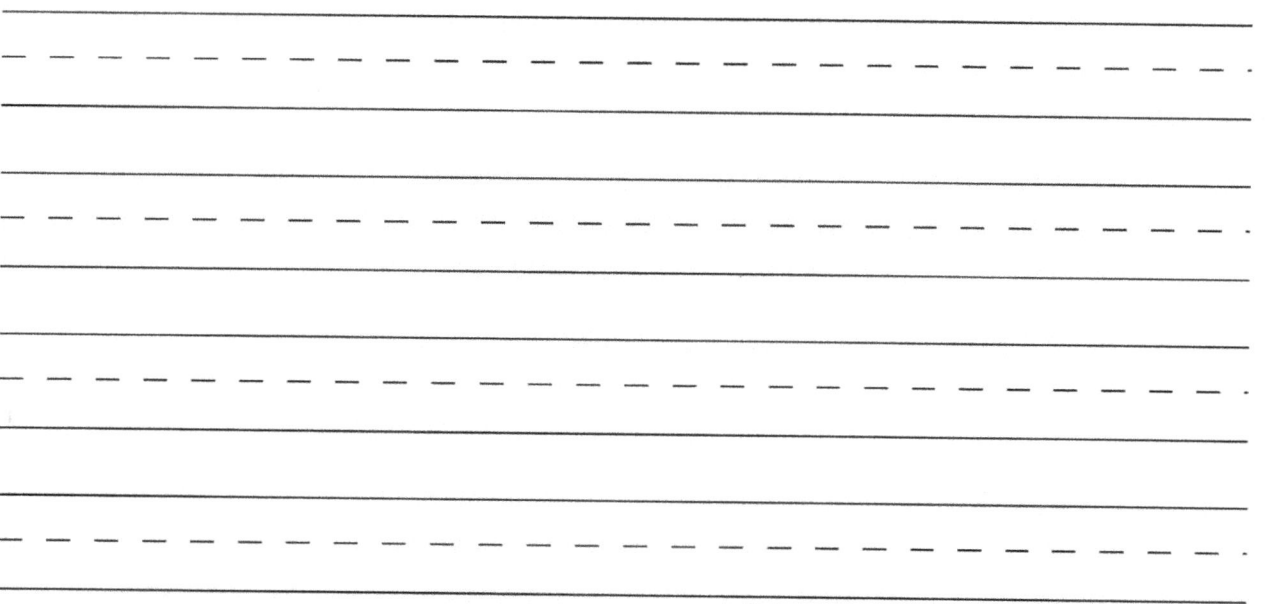

LEARNING TO WRITE UPPER AND LOWERCASE ALPHABET

Now it is time to start learning to write in cursive. When you begin, you will not learn how to write cursive letters in alphabetical order. Instead, you will learn the letters which have similar strokes. Here is how to do this.

1. For each exercise trace and follow the upper and lowercase alphabet at the top of each page using a pencil like the one pictured below.

Cc

2. Practice following the dot-to-dot letters until you are comfortable.

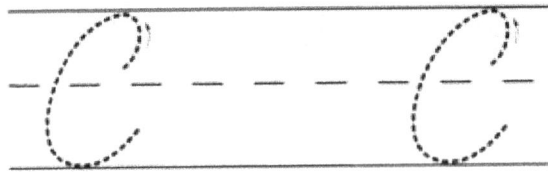

3. In the spaces between the dot-to-dot letters, use that area for independent practice.

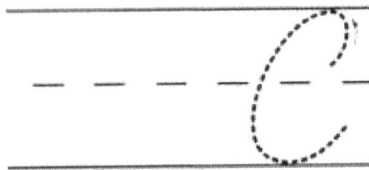

_C_ for cat

Cc

C C C C C

C C C C C

C C C C C

c c c c c

c c c c c

c c c c c

A for apple

$\mathcal{A}a$

a a a a a

a a a a a

a a a a a

a a a a a

a a a a a

a a a a a

D for dog

Dd

D D D D D

D D D D D

D D D D D

d d d d d

d d d d d

d d d d d

G for grapes

Gg

Hh

H for house

H H H H H

H H H H H

H H H H H

h h h h h

h h h h h

h h h h h

$\mathcal{T}t$

$\mathcal{T}$ for tree

$\mathcal{T}$ $\mathcal{T}$ $\mathcal{T}$ $\mathcal{T}$ $\mathcal{T}$

$\mathcal{T}$ $\mathcal{T}$ $\mathcal{T}$ $\mathcal{T}$ $\mathcal{T}$

$\mathcal{T}$ $\mathcal{T}$ $\mathcal{T}$ $\mathcal{T}$ $\mathcal{T}$

t t t t t

t t t t t

t t t t t

P for panda

Pp

E for elephant

Ee

F for flower

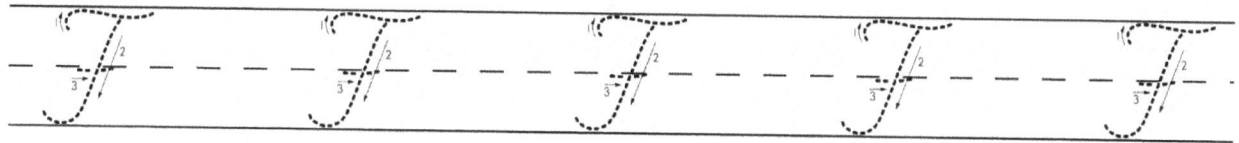

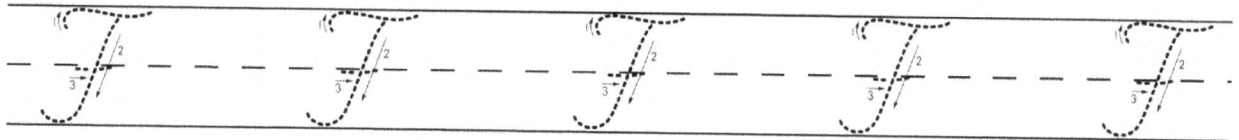

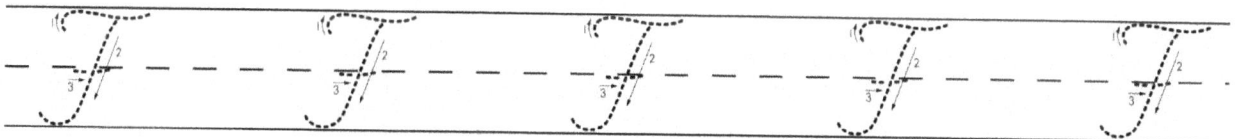

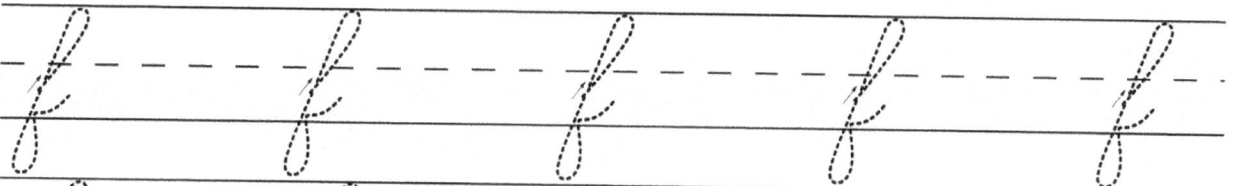

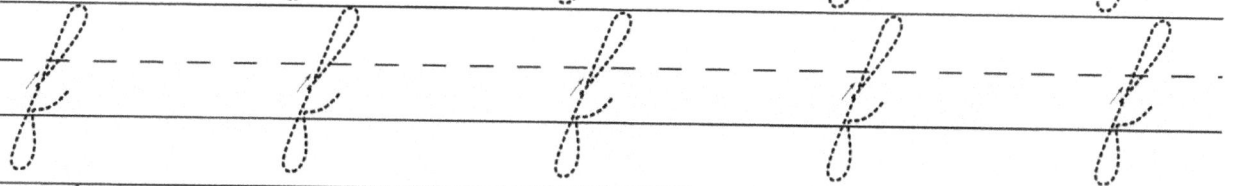

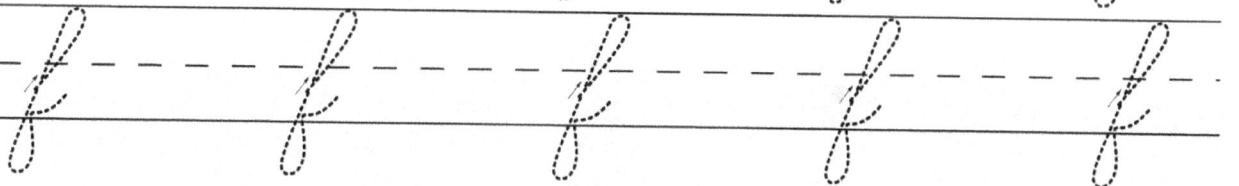

Q q

2 for queen

Q *Q* *Q* *Q* *Q*

Q *Q* *Q* *Q* *Q*

Q *Q* *Q* *Q* *Q*

q *q* *q* *q* *q*

q *q* *q* *q* *q*

q *q* *q* *q* *q*

U for umbrella

Uu

U   U   U   U   U

U   U   U   U   U

U   U   U   U   U

u   u   u   u   u

u   u   u   u   u

u   u   u   u   u

I for igloo

Ii

I   *I*   *I*   *I*   *I*

I   *I*   *I*   *I*   *I*

I   *I*   *I*   *I*   *I*

i   *i*   *i*   *i*   *i*

i   *i*   *i*   *i*   *i*

i   *i*   *i*   *i*   *i*

J for jaguar

Jj

Kk

K for kite

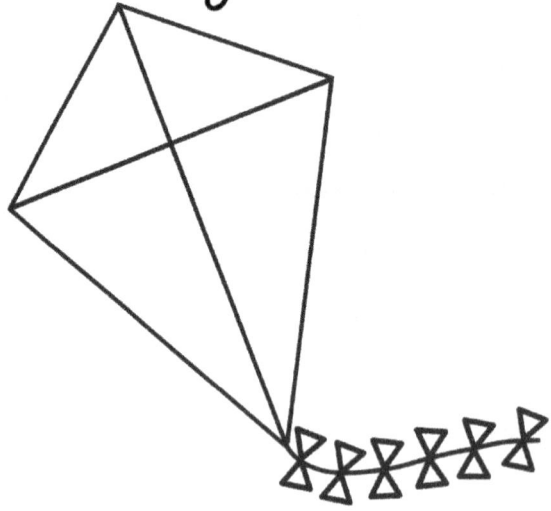

K   K   K   K   K

K   K   K   K   K

K   K   K   K   K

k   k   k   k   k

k   k   k   k   k

k   k   k   k   k

R for ring

Rr

R R R R R

R R R R R

R R R R R

r r r r r

r r r r r

r r r r r

S for square

$\mathcal{S}s$

O for octopus

Oo

O   O   O   O   O

O   O   O   O   O

O   O   O   O   O

o   o   o   o   o

o   o   o   o   o

o   o   o   o   o

B for butterfly

Bb

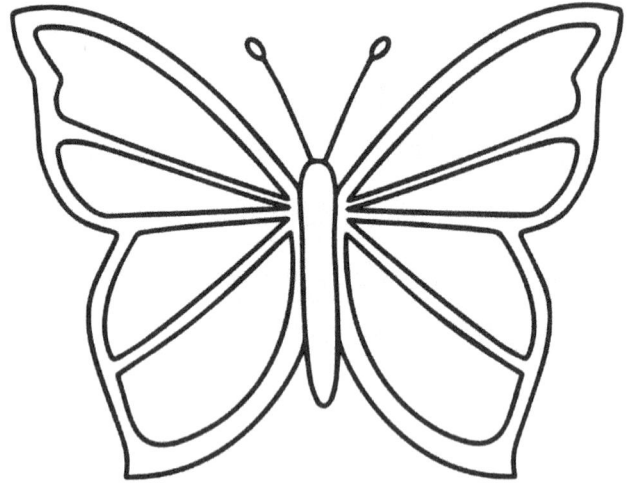

B B B B B

B B B B B

B B B B B

b b b b b

b b b b b

b b b b b

V for vase

Vv

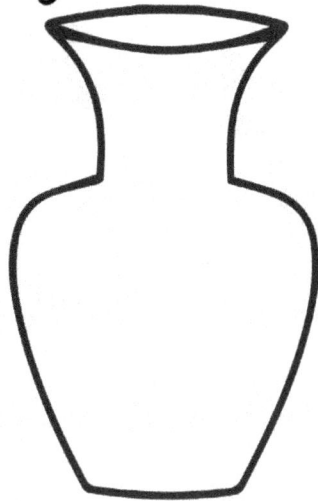

𝒱 𝒱 𝒱 𝒱 𝒱

𝒱 𝒱 𝒱 𝒱 𝒱

𝒱 𝒱 𝒱 𝒱 𝒱

𝓋 𝓋 𝓋 𝓋 𝓋

𝓋 𝓋 𝓋 𝓋 𝓋

𝓋 𝓋 𝓋 𝓋 𝓋

W for waterfall

Ww

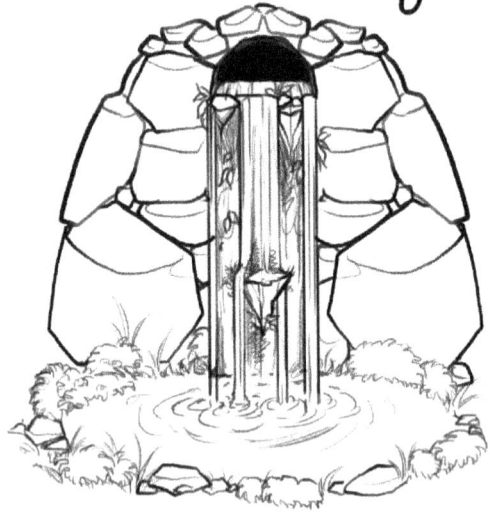

M for monkey

$\mathcal{M}m$

$\mathcal{M}$ $\mathcal{M}$ $\mathcal{M}$ $\mathcal{M}$ $\mathcal{M}$

$\mathcal{M}$ $\mathcal{M}$ $\mathcal{M}$ $\mathcal{M}$ $\mathcal{M}$

$\mathcal{M}$ $\mathcal{M}$ $\mathcal{M}$ $\mathcal{M}$ $\mathcal{M}$

m m m m m

m m m m m

m m m m m

n for nail

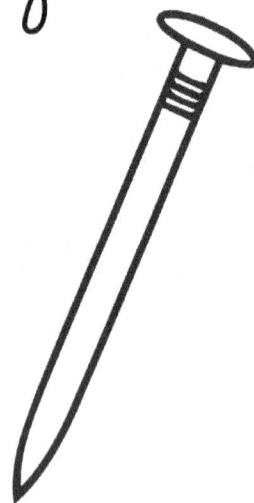

Nn

n n n n n

n n n n n

n n n n n

n n n n n

n n n n n

n n n n n

Yy

Y for yoyo

Y Y Y Y Y

Y Y Y Y Y

Y Y Y Y Y

Y Y Y Y Y

Y Y Y Y Y

Y Y Y Y Y

X for xylophone

Xx

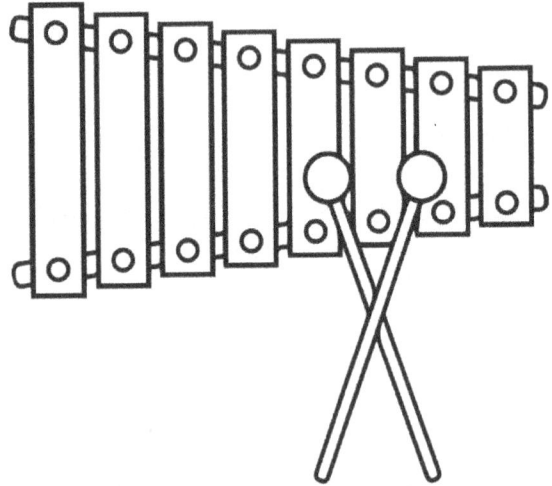

X X X X X

X X X X X

X X X X X

x x x x x

x x x x x

x x x x x

z for zebra

CONNECT THE DOTS

Connect the dots to complete the picture and color it.

MAZE PUZZLE

Help the monkey to find the banana!

COLOR BY NUMBERS

Color the picture by the color numbers listed below.

1. BLUE   4. PURPLE
2. BROWN   5. YELLOW
3. ORANGE   6. GRAY

SPOT THE DIFFERENCE

Find the differences between the two pictures below and color them.

PART 2

Cursive Writing Numbers, Colors, Seasons, Months, and Names

One   one   1

One

one

Two   two   2

Two

two

Three   three   3

Three

three

Four   four   4

Four

four

Five   five   5

Five

five

Six   six   6

Six

six

Seven   seven   7

Seven

seven

Eight   eight   8

Eight

eight

Nine   nine   9

Nine

nine

Ten   ten   10

Ten

ten

Eleven eleven 11

Eleven

eleven

Twelve twelve 12

Twelve

twelve

Thirteen thirteen 13

Thirteen

thirteen

Fourteen fourteen 14

Fourteen

fourteen

Fifteen fifteen 15

Fifteen

fifteen

Sixteen sixteen **16**

Sixteen

sixteen

Seventeen seventeen **17**

Seventeen

seventeen

Eighteen eighteen **18**

Eighteen

eighteen

Nineteen nineteen 19

Nineteen

nineteen

Twenty twenty 20

Twenty

twenty

Thirty thirty 30

Thirty

thirty

Forty   forty   40

Forty

forty

Fifty   fifty   50

Fifty

fifty

Sixty   sixty   60

Sixty

sixty

Seventy   seventy   70

Seventy

seventy

Eighty   eighty   80

Eighty

eighty

Ninety ninety 90

Ninety

ninety

One hundred 100
one hundred

One hundred

one hundred

Are you ready to learn how to write colors in cursive? For each exercise, trace and follow the numbered arrows, practice following the dot-to-dot letters and then complete the independent practice. Ready? Set. Go!

Red   *red*

Red

red

Blue   *blue*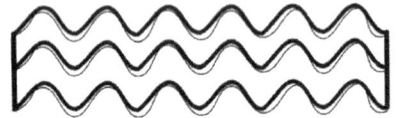

Blue

blue

Yellow   *yellow*

Yellow

yellow

Green green

Green

green

Purple purple

Purple

purple

Orange orange

Orange

orange

Violet violet

Violet

violet

Pink pink

Pink

pink

Brown brown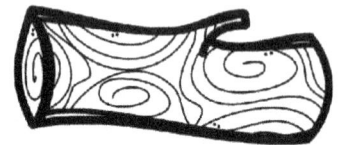

Brown

brown

Black black

Black

black

Teal teal

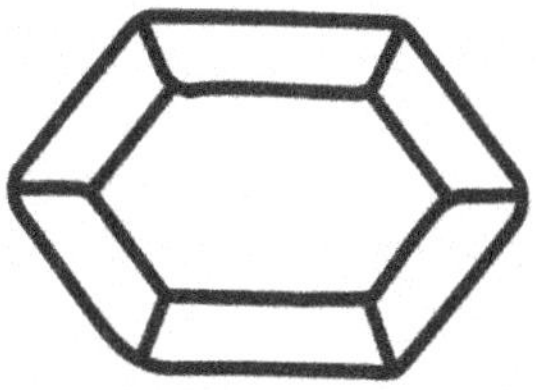

Teal

teal

Gold gold

Gold

gold

Are you ready to learn how to write the seasons and the months of the year in cursive? For each exercise, trace and follow the numbered arrows, practice following the dot-to-dot letters, use the blank areas for independent practice. Ready? Set. Go!

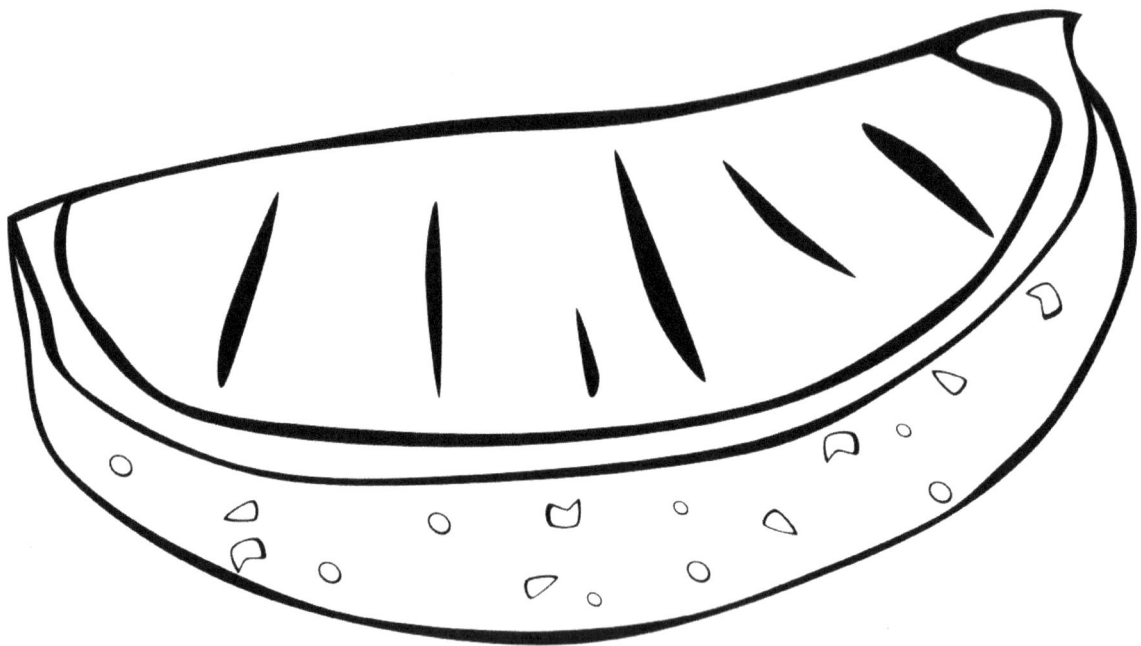

Winter

winter

Winter

winter

Spring

spring

Spring

spring

Summer   summer

Summer

summer

Fall   fall

Fall

fall

January

January   *January*

February

February   *February*

March

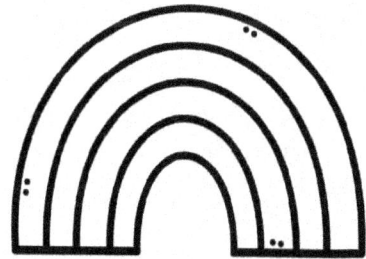

March   *March*

April

April   April

May

May   May

June

June   June

July

July   July

August

August   August

September

September   September

October

October   October

November

November   November

December

December   December

Are you ready to learn how to write your name and other first names in cursive? Begin by printing your first and last name on the line below and then write your name in cursive on the practice lines below. Ready? Set. Go!

_____   _____

First Name   **Last Name**

Sofia

Sofia

Sofia

Aiden

Aiden

Aiden

Roger

Roger

Roger

Amelia

Amelia Amelia

Riley

Riley Riley

Claire

Claire Claire

Noah

Noah — — — — Noah

Ethan

Ethan — — — — Ethan

Carter

Carter — — — — Carter

Ryan

Ryan   Ryan

Julian

Julian   Julian

Caleb

Caleb   Caleb

CONNECT THE DOTS

Connect the dots to complete the picture and color it.

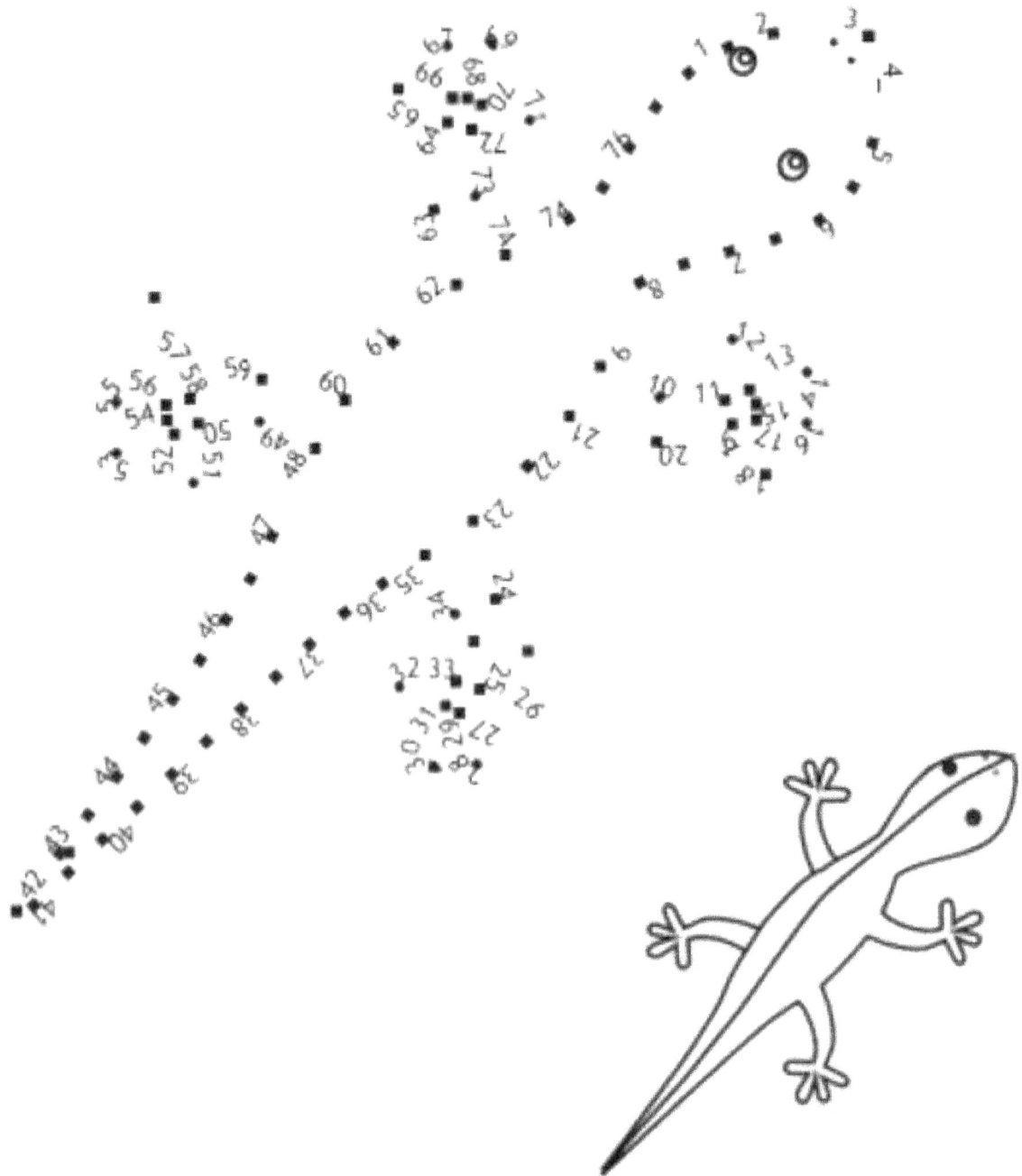

MAZE PUZZLE

Help the girl find a way to reach her balloons!

COLOR BY NUMBERS

Color the picture by the color numbers listed below.

1. GREEN   4. BROWN

2. GRAY   5. PINK

3. ORANGE   6.YELLOW

UNSCRAMBLE THE WORDS

Unscramble the following words that are either a name of a month or a day of the week.

NYOADM   _____

YIFDRA   _____

JUARAYN   _____

FYERABUR   _____

CTEORBO   _____

DEMEECBR   _____

USATGU   _____

AUSNYD   _____

DUSTYEA   _____

AHRCM   _____

ARLIP   _____

ESTREBEPM   _____

PART 3

Cursive Writing Short Words and Sentences

Apple *apple*

Apple

apple

Bee *bee*

Bee

bee

Cake   cake

Cake

cake

Dog   dog

Dog

dog

Eel   eel

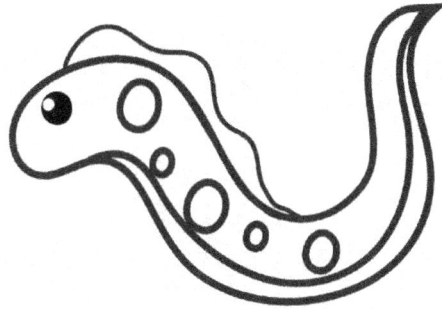

Eel

eel

Frog   frog

Frog

frog

Gate   gate

- - - Gate

- - - gate

Happy   happy

- - - Happy

- - - happy

Ii

I for igloo

Kite

kite

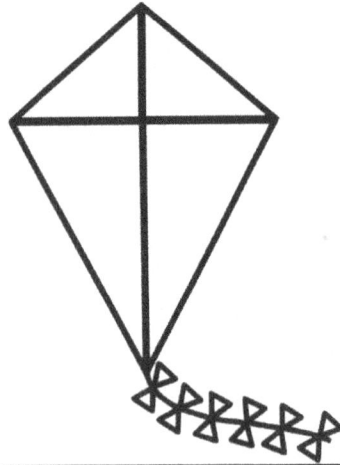

Kite

kite

Lime

lime

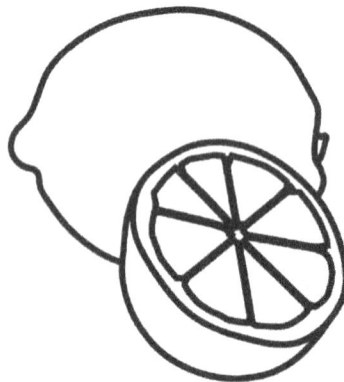

Lime

lime

Milk   *milk*

Milk

milk

Net   *net*

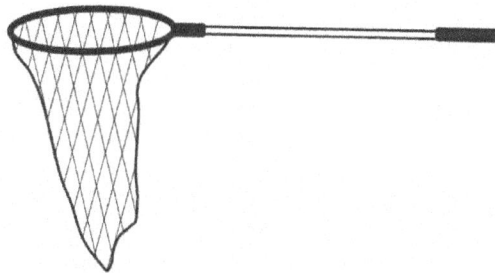

Net

net

Ocean ocean

Ocean

ocean

Pie pie

Pie

pie

Quail   *quail*

Quail

quail

Rooster   *rooster*

Rooster

rooster

$\overset{2}{\underset{1}{S}}\overset{1}{u}\overset{2}{n}\overset{3}{}$ Sun

$\overset{2}{s}\overset{1}{u}\overset{2}{n}\overset{3}{}$ sun

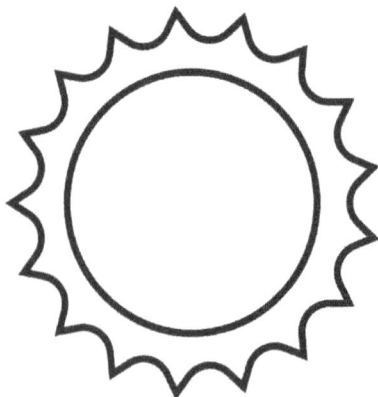

Sun

sun

$\overset{1}{T}\overset{2}{e}\overset{2}{n}\overset{4}{t}$ Tent

$\overset{2}{t}\overset{4}{e}\overset{2}{n}\overset{4}{t}$ tent

Tent

tent

Umbrella umbrella

Umbrella

umbrella

Vase vase

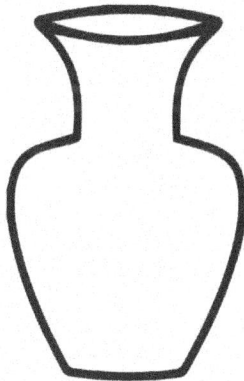

Vase

vase

Whale   *whale*

Whale

whale

X-ray   *x-ray*

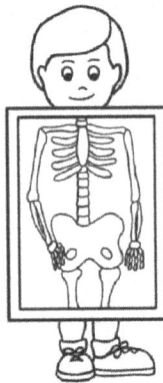

X-ray

x-ray

Yolk

yolk

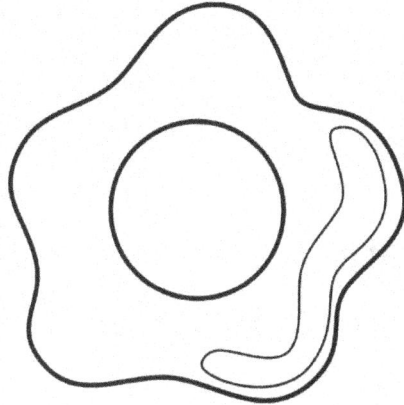

Yolk

yolk

Zoo

Zoo

Zoo

Zoo

Are you ready to learn how to write short sentences in cursive? Remember to follow the numbered arrows. **Ready? Set. Go!**

Apple   apple

Apple

apple

Bee   bee

Bee

bee

Cake   *cake*

Cake

cake

Dog      *dog*

Dog

dog

It snows in the winter.

It snows in the winter.

I love to swim in the summer.

I love to swim in the summer.

Ava and Emily love purple.

Ava and Emily love purple.

Carter and Roger play ball.

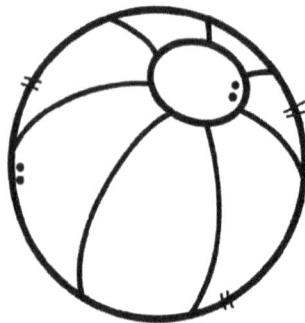

Carter and Roger play ball.

School starts in August.

School starts in August.

I have one brown dog.

I have one brown dog.

I have two orange cats.

I have two orange cats.

The green frog jumps funny.

The green frog jumps funny.

I like cherry pie.

I like cherry pie.

When I am happy, I smile.

When I am happy, I smile.

The rooster crows.

The rooster crows.

The igloo is made of ice.

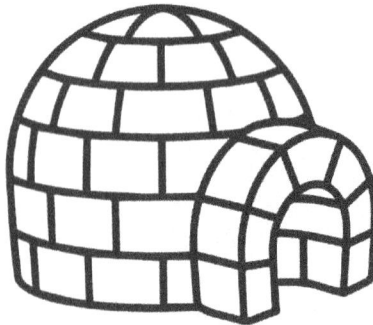

The igloo is made of ice.

I like camping in a tent.

I like camping in a tent.

The kite has many colors.

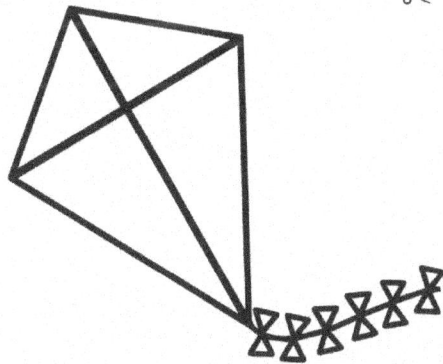

The kite has many colors.

The whale is very large.

The whale is very large.

The zoo is a fun place to visit.

The zoo is a fun place to visit.

Flowers bloom in the spring.

Flowers bloom in the spring.

Ice cream is frozen.

Ice cream is frozen.

I love to eat pizza.

I love to eat pizza.

I like to play in the park.

I like to play in the park.

NOUN CROSSWORD

Complete the crossword puzzle by filling appropriate letters.

I

U

T

L

A

O

CHILD   BIRD
GIRL   APPLE
HOME   POLICE
BOY   STUDY
STORY   SCHOOL
ROOM   YEAR
COOKIE RING
ROAD

CONNECT THE DOTS

Connect the dots to complete the picture and color it for fun.

MAZE PUZZLE

Help the bee to find the flower!

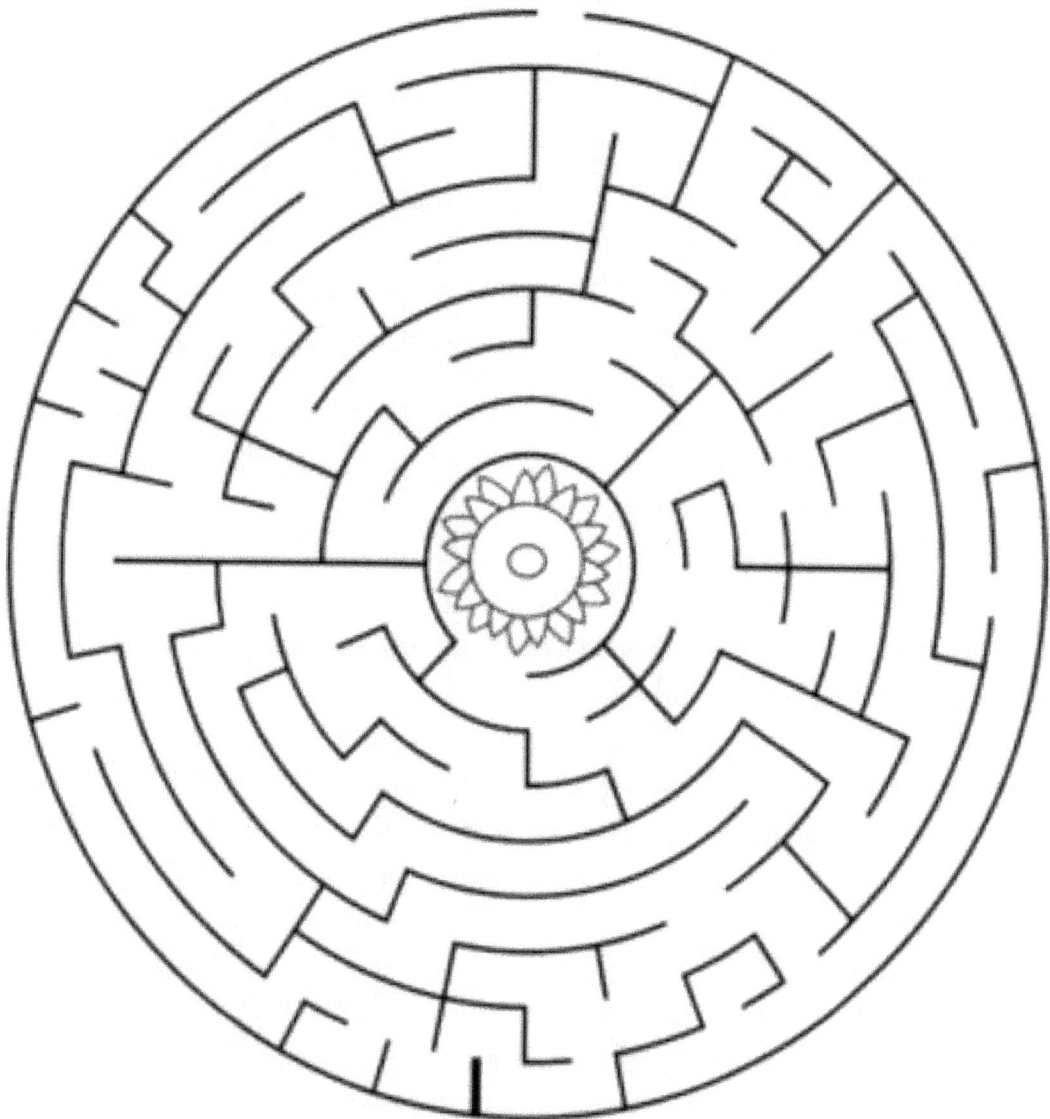

IDENTIFY THE SHAPE

Find and color all squares in the picture below.

OTHER BOOKS BY DR. MELISSA CAUDLE

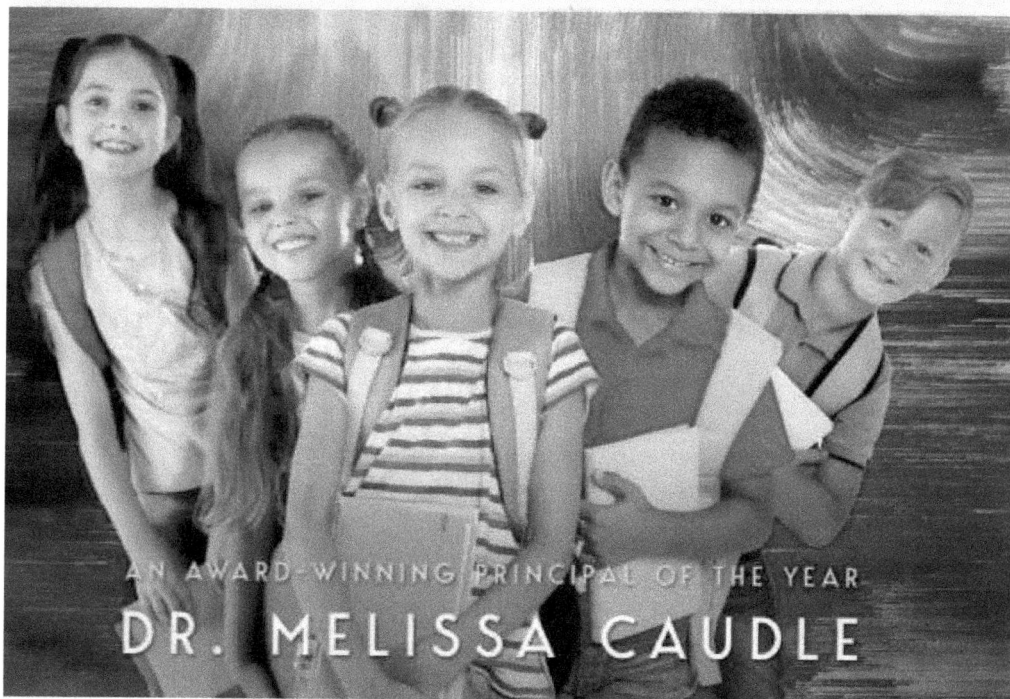

Cursive Beginning
HANDWRITING
THE BIG LINED PAPER
PRACTICE WORKBOOK
Book 2

AN AWARD-WINNING PRINCIPAL OF THE YEAR
DR. MELISSA CAUDLE

AVAILABLE ON AMAZON

TRACING AND WRITING THE CURSIVE ALPHABET in Lower and Uppercase from A - Z for Elementary Kids. — Book 1 — DR. MELISSA CAUDLE

CURSIVE WRITING NUMBERS COLORS, SEASONS, MONTHS, AND NAMES FOR ELEMENTARY KIDS — Book 2 — DR. MELISSA CAUDLE

WRITING SHORT WORDS AND SENTENCES IN CURSIVE FOR ELEMENTARY KIDS — Book 3 — DR. MELISSA CAUDLE

HANDWRITING PRACTICE LINED PAPER CURSIVE FOR ELEMENTARY KIDS — Book 4 — DR. MELISSA CAUDLE

AVAILABLE ON AMAZON

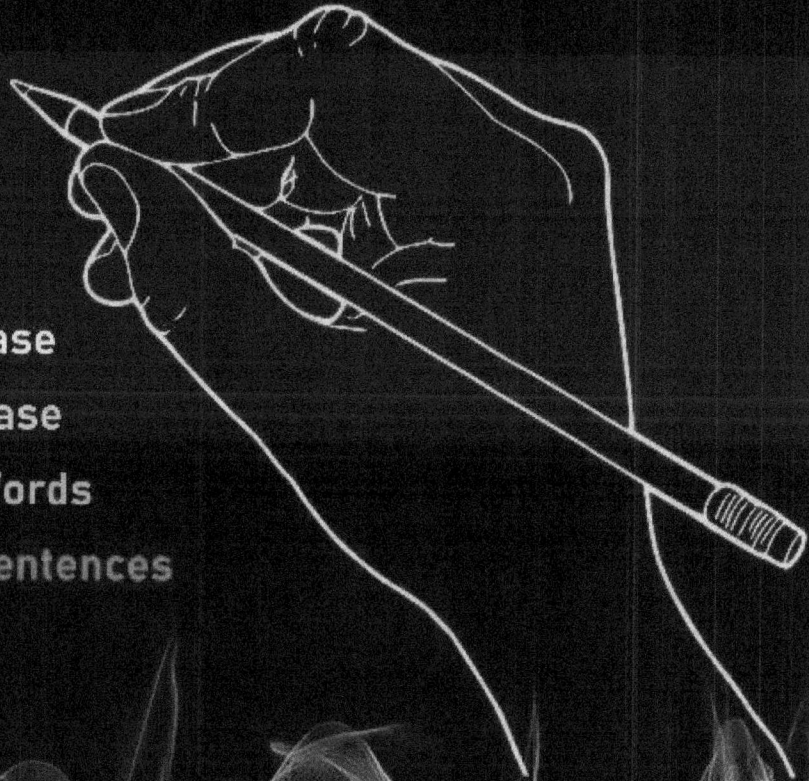

LEARN CURSIVE WRITING FOR TEENS

From A–Z Using Leadership Quotes

- Uppercase
- Lowercase
- Short Words
- Short Sentences

Dr. Melissa Caudle

LEARNING CURSIVE WRITING *for Young Adults*

USING WORDS TO BUILD CONFIDENCE

DR. MELISSA CAUDLE

AWARD CERTIFICATE

Presented to:

_____

For
Completing "The Big Book of Cursive Writing"

DATE:_____

Dr. Melissa Caudle

CONGRATULATIONS

www.ingramcontent.com/pod-product-compliance
Lightning Source LLC
Chambersburg PA
CBHW081256040426
42452CB00014B/2522